This book is the second edition of My Cleanse. Like the author, it has evolved into a fine, velvety wine. All poems from the previous edition are included in chapter one, MY CLEANSE, while her new work is included in chapter two, RED WINE & BLACK INK.

AF416019

My Cleanse: The Red Wine & Black Ink Edition

Lila Love

Published by Lila Love, 2022.

MY CLEANSE: THE RED WINE & BLACK INK EDITION

First edition. December 11, 2022.

Copyright © 2022 Lila Love.

ISBN: 979-8215135006

Written by Lila Love.

Table of Contents

Feelings are not meant to be held in. It's too toxic.
This is my cleanse.

CHAPTER 1
MY CLEANSE

FICTION

Your pages are beginning to bend, corners beginning to tear. After reading you so many times, highlighting the fine print and memorizing each line, you are now so unbelievably clear to my skeptical mind.

You change with each chapter, using pretty words to satisfy my eyes. But now, jumping off the page, are your once, well-hidden, lies.

I now see past your pretty cover. Your inviting preface and happy ending. I've read between the lines, proof read the facts and yes, took careful, descriptive, notes each time.

Now I'm confronting you. I've made my decision, sit and listen.

You're way overdue. I'm sending you back. I thought with you I'd find the genuine truth, but all I found was fiction.

36 SUPERIOR STREET

Letting my curiosity get the best of me, I drove past you today. I wanted to see what had become of your dark red bricks that held you together. The dark red bricks that penetrated my eyes and so often filled mine with fear.

I was surprised and a little envious to see what you had become. To see how perfect your new appearance seemed to be. My nightmare had somehow become someone else's dream.

The once white chipped fence was now covered with a new glistening white paint. The once bare trees that I played under, alone, were filled with an arrangement of beautiful leaves. The grass so green, the yard so clean, and all I have of you, are the saddest memories.

But you belong to someone else now. You're no longer mine. You're no longer filled with hatred. You're filled with love. Please, leave them with happy memories that you couldn't leave with me.

MARCH

The year passes without you, but you overtake the color of our present.

Stay away.

SEVEN DAYS

Day one, I will notice you.
Day two, I'll give you the time of day.
And if you make it to day three,

I

might

be

falling.

But by day four, I'll let reality hit.
Smiles will fade by day five.
The flame will only be an uncomfortable burning by day
six. And on day seven,

I'll

finally

say

goodbye.

GLASS

Glitter or glass,
    he said I was mad.
    Red or black, sometimes blue.
    Because I could never trust you, I yelled.
    You hit.
    I would retaliate.
    Make up.
    Glitter again, until glass.

ALREADY DEAD

What if I can't ever escape you?
    I only seem to forget you when I can find you.
    Right now, I can't find you.
    I'm afraid this means I'm already dead.

TEXAS

You were Texas, I was New York.
>   For a short while you were the sun that warmed my heart.
>   Naïve and young,
>   I gave you everything I could for a while.
>   And you kept me safe from the demons that lurked.
>   You showed me charming and safe,
>   but you couldn't keep the truth at bay.
>   Your demons fought until one night the sun set on Texas,
>   and the darkness gave you away.

I'M LEAVING

Like an ocean, enormous, overwhelming.
    Sometimes calm and enticing.
    But you can't control it.
    I need security, something you can't give me.
    Stability.
    I'm playing Russian roulette,
    becoming something I'm not.
    Some days you are the calm before the storm, and I feel
    most days, I have become the storm.
    I'm leaving.

STILL A GHOST

I did not fail you.

I survived you.

I escaped you, but not completely.

You are still a ghost that lingers, intrigues my mind, but haunts me.

Some might say, because of this, you win. That may be so.

But trust me when I say you will never get a chance to beat me again.

METAPHOR

I write best in metaphors. So, you will be the sun and I will be the tree.

I loved the warmth and your light. You were loyal. You were predictable.

I rose and set with you. I was no longer standing and growing alone.

But just as we were taught, everything is best in moderation.

So were we.

And so were you.

BEAUTIFULLY BROKEN

"You are broken," he said. And this time I replied, "yes, I am."

But aren't all the best things broken?

Let me shine through the cracks, learn from these dents and heal from these bruises.

I use these experiences as guidance. So, whatever you throw my way, I can navigate through those barriers.

And with grace and courage I will rise above,

beautifully broken.

WHY

I think you look at the world and see yourself in the center.
Did I describe you perfectly?
I can't be exactly right, of course. Unless you agree.
Did I interpret that correctly?
You are the sun. You shine the light. We watch the show.
Well, let me be the first to ask,
why can't the sun set more quickly?

ANXIETY

These thoughts in my head like the grey in November.

Trying to breathe under water, the lifeguards always one step behind.

And when I reach the bottom, there's never any quiet.

It just starts again, and it's a scary thing.

A nightmare without closure.

A wound that can't mend.

But I get up each day, and I just try again.

EXIT 49

The sun was setting. It was a warm fall night. We were both driving north down the highway. As we passed exit 49, I couldn't take it anymore. The truth came out. I told you I didn't love you, our time had run out.

You didn't look at me as the tears ran down my face. You sat silent the rest of the drive. We said goodbye, and you moved on with your life.

I couldn't hold on. Letting go set us free. I couldn't even try. You deserved better and I needed to breathe.

This door is closed and the next one hasn't opened yet. But if I'm fine, why am I still here at exit 49?

You haven't spoke to me since last night, and I can't remember anything past exit 49. I heard you moved away and you're doing fine.

I'm still waiting for the grass to turn green on this side. Still can't move past exit 49.

Regret is a lonely place to be, but sometimes it's where we need to be.

BROKEN BIRD

She was confident but he was jealous.

Her colors were bright but he dulled them.

He couldn't compete so he broke her.

Little by little, piece by piece, she was a bird locked in a cage with clipped wings and no song to sing.

Yet everyone asked, why don't you just leave?

SLITHER

You slither like a snake, swiftly and carefully positioning yourself around my neck, squeezing until I can no longer breathe.

And just as the light begins to dim, I'm realizing all too late, the moment I thought I became the predator,

I was actually the prey.

LILY

We would have named you Lily.

I ask myself how I can miss something or someone that was never there?

How can something be missing when it never existed?

But never the less, the pain remains and the tears fall so effortlessly.

Some say it gets better. Others just roll their eyes, but it's okay. It's hard to understand something that doesn't make sense.

And it still isn't completely clear to me.

I just know, we would have named you Lily.

CHAPTER 2
RED WINE AND BLACK INK

RED WINE & BLACK INK

Red wine.
Black ink.
Just a few of my favorite things.
An untold story,
Ready to come to life.
And if it brings you to your knees,
It was worth the anticipation,
And all my sleepless night.

CONGRATULATIONS, YOU'RE FAT

No one congratulates you for gaining weight.
Interactions become like awkward elevator rides.
A bad accident, we stare, when we should look away.
You eat alone.
The guilt, unbearable, when you stare into the mirror.
So, we stop counting our blessings,
and count calories and carbs instead.
When did the refrigerator become a prison?
The scale, a warden.
Utensils, weapons.
What we weigh, our worth.
You're fat, congratulations.

ALCOHOL, THE NARCISSIST

Alcohol, you are, without a doubt, a narcissist.
Your inviting smile and warmth draw us close.
Oh, the fun we have, it always looks so
glamorous on the outside.
We dance, we laugh, we are bullet proof.
You're like liquid magic. You give us courage.
You take away all of our problems.
But sadly, the illusion never lasts.
The clock must strike twelve.
The friends we thought we made were make believe, merely,
pumpkins.
And we wake up, alone, with one less shoe.
As we try to piece together the puzzle
of what happened the night before.
We vow to never partake again.
But then minutes, hours, and days pass.
And there you are,
with that same smile and warm embrace,
And our carriage awaits...

WINTER RAIN

And life just goes on.
I can't pause this moment.
I can't catch my breath.
I want to stay frozen in place, like this winter rain,
After it hits the pavement and freezes.
There is no magic.
No ruby red slippers.
We play the cards we are dealt,
And create our own happy endings.

EULOGY

No one can absolve you of your actions,
But you try.
All the deflecting and pointing you do.
Are your fingers black and blue?
Are you unable to recall the details,
Because you snorted all those lines?
Do flashes of the truth haunt your psyche?
Either way, I bet you sleep like a baby.
I guess we will get the last laugh,
When this becomes your eulogy.

HUMAN

Scars.
Signs of living.
Good or tragic,
I've lived.
No one can take that away from me.

CLEAN

I bet you washed me off so easily.
To you, your hands are clean.
I spend my life haunted.
My emotional responses to everything,
Escalated,
Theatrical,
Because your gift of trauma remains.
It didn't wash off me quite so easily.
Like a rash,
it spread,
and has infected every area of my life.
While you, remain,
"clean. "

CHECK MATE

Blind betrayal.
Bending the truth.
A crisis of conscious,
Not knowing what to do.
So I turn to my muse.
What would she say?
Her advice, I suspect, would be,
Keep your secrets, they are your greatest asset.
Turn your feelings into the biggest payday of your life.
Fuck them.
Check mate.

BLIND EYE

A glass of red.
A night of mourning.
A morning of regret.
My mind like a chalkboard;
Brainstorming reasons we didn't work out.
People change?
Plans get lost?
Full moon?
Or the least possible if all...
we just didn't connect....

POISON

I watch the lies drip...
Like honey off your lips.
I hate the way you make me feel, and still, without force,
I swallow each lie.
Letting it burn the whole way down.
You taste sweet but harsh. Bitter.
A drink too strong.
800 proof.
And still, without persuasion,
I let you poison all of me.

SURRENDER

Running, Hiding, giving in.
Escaping without closure.
I am not letting you win.
Here's the truth.
Take it all.
I am not running, hiding, or giving in anymore.

INDULGENCE

Made you a cake,
And brought you a fork.
Realizing, that I,
Knew your motives, all along.

ACCEPTANCE

Each day dinner is served at 5 o clock.
Per his request.
Lately, he gets home later and later.
She waits, patiently.
And greets him at the door, no questions asked.
But tonight, it's even later.
At 6:46 he arrives.
And to no one's surprise , their dinner is cold.
And the story unfolds in his eyes. She watches carefully.
The lies, the deceit and betrayal.
She's only second best, but still his wife.
He waits for her to ask.
But she just smiles and pulls up a chair.
They eat in silence, and he knows what she knows.
But she never asks.
She will never ask.

ENCORE

Another knife in the back.
Another slap in the face.
Thanks for nothing.
I will be on my way.
Your smile, so sweet.
So fake.
Your words like sugar.
Syrup drips from your face.
You're like a tick that attaches and feeds, and you grow and
grow, infecting all that you touch.
Your show, so viciously designed.
When the encore plays out,
I will be standing by,
Patiently waiting for the real you to arrive.

BREAK MY FALL

If you were to separate
Every piece of my heart,.
You'd find your face
Imprinted on each one.
I ran.
You found me.
I jumped,
You caught me.
Like a hero of thc hcart,
You break my fall.
You break my fall.

HOPELESS

Fat. Fat. Fat.
I'm sick with sadness.
A knot I can't untangle.
And obsession bigger than me.
Hollow parcels of hope try to make me believe
It gets better. It doesn't matter.
So, I watch the embers of my confidence burn as you stare at
what's become of me.
Restless, faded.
A version of myself I can't come back from.

MY LEGACY

If I teach you anything.
Let it be resilience.
People will come and go, and that's ok.
You get to choose who stays.
Not everyone will love you. And that's ok.
You won't love everyone either.
You are a unique soul who
will connect to those who matter.
Priorities form with experience and time.
And you have so much of that on your side.
So be kind to each other and yourselves,
As you dance around and through, life.

INVISIBLE

If I didn't call you,
This conversation would never happen.
You put forth zero effort.
And I can't take the pressure,
So I'm not giving in
So, no, this conversation is never going to happen.

SAME SHIT. NEW YEAR.

Template.
White canvas.
January 1st.
Monday.
New year.
New day.
So many opportunities to recreate
Who we are.
But we complain and remain,
The same.

RESILIENCE

Serve up some smiles,
And I will choose one to wear.
Pass me the laughter.
I will indulge in happiness
To hide these tears.
Slice me some freedom and
Top it with directions,
So I can run far away from here.
Please don't pass me anymore heartache,
I believe that I have had my fair share.
No, I'm quite full of pain.
But I won't cash in my stars just yet.
I will unglue them one by one and
Let them paint the truth.
Karma will sort out the rest of it.

CUBIC ZIRCONIA

You make me feel like a fake diamond,
The dirt beneath your feet.
A wine stain.
And I think I'm being generous,
because I'd like to say some vile shit.
But I choose grace.
Words unspoken and unwritten can be denied easier.

DEAD ROOTS

She smells sweet like flowers.
Roses, maybe.
But she's dead inside.

MERCY

You destroyed me.
I mean it with every sense and
being of that word.
You obliterated me.
Found my weakest point and attacked.
Smelled blood and festered.
I have nothing left.
My last request;
Mercy.

FINALITY

Regret.
Such a powerful word.
A feeling that can replace everything.
And erase the happy things.
It's a Wednesday night.
7:58.
And I'm trying to remember the reasons I gave it all away.
The life I made.
Miracles.
And you were in safest in my heart.
My womb.
God's gift.
And I traded it all in,
for nothing.

HOLLOW

The disconnect.
I walk it,
everyday.
It's path,
hollow.
It's heart,
empty.
But I fake it.
I smile.
And give what is expected.
No one wants the truth.
So nice nothings it is.

SHAME

I held my head in shame.
But you knew better.
And so did she.
But oh the art of corruption,
And manipulation,
And it's seductive nature.
You fooled me.
But I thought that I was to blame.
How dare you.
She closed the door.
And I let you involve me in your sick and twisted world.
And here I am, today,
Still fucking ashamed.

INFAMY

I wanted crimson red.
But you, you were more mauve.
Safe.
I couldn't find the passion in our dance.
So I lost both shoes on purpose and waited, impatiently, for
the clock to strike twelve, then ran.
Some days I regret my cowardliness.
But if things were different, you may have never met the love
of your life.

MAKE UP

Brush my hair.
Cover my face with foundation,
hide my secrets.
Flaws.
Next the eyes.
Turn them into gleaming beauties.
No one wants to hear about the sadness
and pain behind them.
Get yourself together.
And did you know?
Your tears make you weak.
So apply that rosy nude blush.
Paint your lips an appropriate shade of red.
Subdued.
It's a facade.
And I'm the worst fake of them all.

JOHNNY & JUNE

Our aesthetic, like a vintage Polaroid.
The glow of a candle.
Our aroma, home, that's us.
Christmas lights.
The magic of every season.
But this love doesn't come without a price.
The adversity we've faced;
And with blind faith we fought,
but with realistic expectations.
We know there's more to come.
But you take my hand and watch as
I place the stars above us.
And you are our moon, our Johnny.
And I will always be, your June.

IMPOSTER

Welcome to my pity party
Where I overthink and undervalue everything I say,
They say it takes a village,
To build us up, but to also tear us down.
Word by word, I set myself on fire, and they gather around to
wine and dine in the warmth of my self-sabotage.
They prey on the weak and get high off my insecurities.
But the worst part of all this disaster, is that I served myself up
on a silver platter, all along knowing, being your own worst
enemy in a village this small,
is not for the faint of heart.

NAÏVE

Words flowing like cheap Cabernet, they keep pouring.
Liquid courage.
It goes down so easy,
and like poison the next day.
But tonight, with merlot color glasses,
I set the stage.
Only the second drink in my hand,
and I spill all of my secrets to anyone
willing to listen.
I make friends with everyone and leave with none.

WAR

No vacancy.
No room.
No hospitality,
And no choice.
Every door must close to win this fight.
The enemy is after everything.
My heart,
My spirit,
My light.
And the battlefield, my mind.
This fight cannot be fought with honor.
If I follow the rules, I'm sure to lose.
So with blood I fight until they surrender with white.
And I will reclaim what I came for,
My life.

MOCKERY

I didn't know until it was too late,
I walk with snakes,
with faces disguised as friends.
My toxic trait,
Generosity.
Rose colored glasses of pure positivity.
Others tried to warn me,
But I didn't listen.
Then piece by piece, they swallowed me whole.
And now, my head stone reads;
Here rests the weak, pitied and naive.
We told you so.

FAKE

Is anyone as fake as me?
I smile, but on the inside, I'm wondering how,
I will make it until tomorrow.
My heart is weeping.
Anxiety,
a real life monster,
the main villain in this story.
Its multiple attempts at killing off the main character has
failed so far.
But I can't fight forever.

PEOPLE PLEASER

Would you have jumped off a bridge if they did too?
Yes, I would've.
The need for acceptance is a
Dangerous game.
No freedom.
You give all your stars away.
Pockets empty,
You leave with nothing.

SWEET NOTHINGS

He says I'm a loose cannon.
It's too late for me to grow up.
The house echoes with his words.
No one is safe from his rigid and icy outbursts.
So we sit, listen and wonder,
Did we really deserve this?

FIRE

Her sun has risen and set with you,
from day one.
The blood sweat and tears and years she has given to support
the ones she loves.
She sees a life she has been longing for.
Your view, stability that she provides.
But the bridge has been built.
The path is paved,
All road signs point forward.
Watch her set this trail on fire.

SMALL TOWN PAPARAZZI

Oh, the small town paparazzi,
they have made so many of us famous.
They decorate these streets infamously using our names like
they are stringing Christmas lights for all to see.
And they guard their castle, the local watering hole, with their
plastic pitch forks and liquid courage.
They prey on weakness and dare us to enter.
But without us, they have nothing.
No extracurriculars.
A lonely and pathetic existence.
And that must be a hard pill to swallow.
So, should we thank them for our
15 minutes of fame?
Reward them with our presence?
Give them more to talk about?
I could throw my starlight on the floor and watch their eyes
turn green with envy every night.
But unfortunately for them,
there will be no show tonight,
because unlike them,
I happen to have a nice life.

Thank you for reading My Cleanse: The Red Wine and Black Ink Edition. If you can, please consider leaving a review where you purchased your book.

About the Author

Lila Love was born and raised in upstate New York. She holds a bachelor's in psychology and a master's in human services with a special concentration in counseling studies. Lila served as a substance abuse counselor for ten years and earned her CASAC in 2009. Currently, Lila works as a probation officer for her county. She married in 2009 and now lives in the Village of Theresa, in upstate New York, where she serves her community as a trustee. Lila was elected in 2021. She has four children, Connor, Lucy, Charlie, and Henry.

Read more at https://www.facebook.com/groups/lovepublications.